Rule

1

When you can't see because of the crowd, climb a tree.

Luke 19:2-10
The story of Zacchaeus.

Live more simply.
Give away what you do not need.

Matthew 6:11
Give us today our daily bread.

Ignore petty gripes.

Matthew 5:5
Blessed are the meek, for they will inherit the earth.

Never lose hope.

1 Corinthians 13:7
[Love] always hopes.

Accept constructive criticism.

Proverbs 19:20
Listen to advice and accept instruction, and in the end you will be wise.

Rule
6

Allow your children to debate.
They will learn important skills:
listening, reasoning, cooperation,
and compromise.

Matthew 5:9
Blessed are the peacemakers, for they will be called sons of God.

Rule
7

Allow your children to suffer
the consequences of poor behavior.

Luke 15:11-31
The story of the prodigal son.

"Carpe diem:"
a great name for a goldfish—
and not a bad thought.

Matthew 6:34
*Therefore do not worry about tomorrow, for tomorrow will worry about itself.
Each day has enough trouble of its own.*

Be an optimist.

Philippians 3:20
And we eagerly await a Savior.

Keep a family scrapbook. Record the usual and unusual events: baking cookies, raking leaves, singing around the piano.

Philippians 1:3
I thank my God every time I remember you.

Play fair.

Proverbs 29:14
If a king judges the poor with fairness, his throne will always be secure.

Improve.

2 Peter 3:18
*But grow in the grace and knowledge
of our Lord and Savior Jesus Christ.*

Pray.
Always and everywhere.

1 Thessalonians 5:17
Pray continually.

Mind your own business.

Proverbs 26:17
Like one who seizes a dog by the ears is a passer-by who meddles in a quarrel not his own.

Live beneath your means.

Philippians 4:12
I have learned the secret of being content.

3 4 5 6 7 8 9

Define appropriate behavior
for yourself
and your children.

Proverbs 29:17
Discipline your son, and he will give you peace, he will bring delight to your soul.

When someone is away from home, leave the light on.

Luke 15:11-31
The story of the prodigal son.

Grieve when you must.

Matthew 5:3
Blessed are those who mourn, for they will be comforted.

Rule
19

Watch the night sky on August 11. Count how many meteors you see.

Psalm 19:1
The heavens declare the glory of God.

Rule

20

Shovel the snow off your neighbors' driveway before they get home from work.

Matthew 6:3
*Do not let your left hand know what your right is doing,
so that your giving may be in secret.*

Ask for directions.

Jeremiah 6:16
Ask where the good way is, and walk in it.

Read poetry.
It awakens the soul.

Psalm 23

Volunteer.

Hebrews 13:16
And do not forget to do good and to share with others.

Memorize a Bible verse.
Engrave it on your heart.

Psalm 119:11
I have hidden your word in my heart.

Cancel cable. Read instead.

Revelation 1:3
Blessed is the one who reads the words of this prophecy, and blessed are those who hear it and take to heart what is written in it, because the time is near.

Write a note of encouragement to your pastor.

1 Thessalonians 4:18
Therefore encourage each other.

Rule
27

Create a family flag
complete with symbols
for each family member.

Psalm 68:6
God sets the lonely in families.

Visit the sick
(but keep your visits short).

Matthew 25:36
I was sick and you looked after me.

Learn from your mistakes.

Luke 15:17
*When [the prodigal son]came to his senses, he said . . .
"I will set out and go back to my father."*

To see clearly, change your wiper blades.

Matthew 5:8
Blessed are the pure in heart, for they shall see God.

Ducks fly in a V for a purpose. Be able to work together as a team.

Philippians 2:4
*Each of you should look not only to your own interests,
but also to the interests of others.*

Rule
32

Take a day off
to recharge your batteries.

Psalm 62:1
My soul finds rest in God alone.

Set goals and know your objectives.

Philippians 4:13
I can do everything through him who gives me strength.

Be honest.

Proverbs 24:26
An honest answer is like a kiss on the lips.

Learn to play an instrument.

Psalm 108:1
I will . . . make music with all my soul.

Do more than you are asked to do.

Matthew 5:41
If someone forces you to go one mile, go with him two miles.

Rule
37

Visit the Grand Canyon.

Psalm 93:2
Your throne was established long ago; you are from all eternity.

Make a list.

Proverbs 24:27
Finish your outdoor work and get your fields ready;
after that, build your house.

Learn a second language.

Proverbs 2:6
And from his mouth come knowledge and understanding.

Rule
40

Realize that money is
only green paper.
You can't eat it, wear it, or live in it.
So why horde it?

1 Timothy 6:10
The love of money is a root of all kinds of evil.

Never become intoxicated.

Philippians 1:27
*Whatever happens, conduct yourself
in a manner worthy of the gospel of Christ.*

Occasionally leave the circle
of your own kind.

Matthew 5:47
And if you greet only your brothers, what are you doing more than others?

Keep it to yourself.

Proverbs 26:20
Without wood a fire goes out; without gossip a quarrel dies down.

Once in a while be alone.
Collect your thoughts.

Mark 1:35
Jesus got up, left the house and went off to a solitary place.

Face your fears.

Exodus 3 and 4
The story of Moses' return to Egypt to ask Pharoah for Israel's release.

Accept help when you need it.

Ruth 2:9
*Boaz said to Ruth, "And whenever you are thirsty,
go and get a drink from the water jars."*

Be loyal.

Ruth 1:16
Where you go I will go, and where you stay I will stay.

Leave the beach cleaner than you found it.

Psalm 24:1
The earth is the LORD's, and everything in it.

Rule
49

Age gracefully.

1 Corinthians 13:11
When I became a man, I put childish ways behind me.

Rule
50

Never underestimate the power of the Holy Spirit.

Romans 5:5
God has poured out his love into our hearts by the Holy Spirit.

Cherish happy times.

Ecclesiastes 7:14
When times are good, be happy.

Just do it.

James 1:23–24
Anyone who listens to the word but does not do what it says is like a man who looks at his face in a mirror and, after looking at himself, goes away and immediately forgets what he looks like.

If it's important, speak up.

Proverbs 31:9
Speak up and judge fairly; defend the rights of the poor and needy.

Cultivate one great friendship.

John 15:13
Greater love has no one than this, that he lay down his life for his friends.

Monitor your television habits.

1 John 2:15
Do not love the world.

Be a child for as long as you can.
Then, grow up.

Philippians 3:15
All of us who are mature should take such a view of things.

Rule
57

Limit worry to ten minutes a day.

Philippians 4:6
Do not be anxious about anything.

Be humble.

Matthew 5:3
Blessed are the poor in spirit, for theirs is the kingdom of heaven.

Take comfort in this fact:
This, too, shall pass.

Revelation 21:4
*He will wipe every tear from their eyes. There will be no more death
or mourning or crying or pain.*

Rule
60

Stand amazed at Niagara Falls.

Psalm 93:4
*Mightier than the thunder of great waters, mightier than the breakers of the sea—
the LORD on high is mighty.*

Rule
61

Be polite.
Say "please," "thank you," and
"excuse me" often.

1 Thessalonians 5:15
Always try to be kind to each other.

Stick to your budget.

1 Corinthians 16:2
Each of you should set aside a sum of money in keeping with your income.

Live your faith as a banner,
not as a top-secret file.

Matthew 5:14
You are the light of the world. A city on a hill cannot be hidden.

Show mercy.

Matthew 5:7
Blessed are the merciful, for they will be shown mercy.

Recycle.

Isaiah 51:6
*Lift up your eyes to the heavens, look at the earth beneath;
the heavens will vanish like smoke, the earth will wear out like a garment.*

Rule

66

To have tulips in the spring, plant bulbs in the fall.

James 5:7
*See how the farmer waits for the land to yield its valuable crop
and how patient he is for the autumn and spring rains.*

Set Sunday apart.

Exodus 20:8
Remember the Sabbath Day by keeping it holy.

Take an interest in the welfare of others.

Philippians 2:20
I have no one else like [Timothy], who takes a genuine interest in your welfare.

Rule 69

"Cinderella" is a fairy tale.
If you want your marriage to live
happily ever after, base it on
something greater than shoe size.

Psalm 127:1
Unless the LORD builds the house, its builders labor in vain.

Decide to have a good time at your in-laws'.

Hebrews 12:14
Make every effort to live in peace.

Love your spouse's family.

Ruth 1:16
Your people will be my people.

Rule
75

Eat your vegetables.
She was right again.

Proverbs 12:15
A wise man listens to advice.

Appreciate your parents.
They are with you only a short time.

Exodus 20:12

Honor your father and your mother,
so that you may live long in the land
the LORD your God is giving you.

Bite your tongue.

Psalm 141:3

Set a guard over my mouth, O Lord.

Appreciate your children. They are with you only a short time.

Psalm 127:3
Sons are a heritage from the Lord, children a reward from him.

Use tact.

1 Corinthians 13:5
[Love] is not rude.

Forgive.

Matthew 6:14
*For if you forgive men when they sin against you,
your heavenly Father will also forgive you.*

Then forget.

1 Corinthians 13:5
[Love] keeps no record of wrongs.

Rule 82

Worship with God's people regularly.

Habakkuk 2:20
The LORD is in his holy temple; let all the earth be silent before him.

Smile.

Philippians 2:18
So you . . . should be glad and rejoice with me.

Laugh.
Everyday.

Psalm 126:2
Our mouths were filled with laughter.

Socrates said it well: Know thyself.

1 Kings 9:4
Walk before me in integrity of heart.

Jesus said it better: Know God.

John 10:14
I know my sheep and my sheep know me.

Do your best.

2 Peter 3:14
Make every effort to be found spotless.

Do it with enthusiasm.

Colossians 3:23
Whatever you do, work at it with all your heart.

Rule

89

Visit other houses of worship.
Marvel at the variety of ways
we can praise our God.

1 Chronicles 15:28
. . .with shouts, with the sounding of rams' horns and trumpets, and of cymbals, and the playing of lyres and harps.

Call an old friend.

Philippians 4:10
I rejoice greatly in the Lord that at least you have renewed your concern for me.

Better yet, write.
Letters are our truest history.

Philippians 3:1
It is no trouble for me to write the same things to you again.

Rule 92

Everyday do something you hate to do. Balance your checkbook or scrub the shower tiles. It builds character.

Romans 5:3-4
Suffering produces perseverance; perseverance, character; and character, hope.

Confront only out of love.

Luke 17:3
If your brother sins, rebuke him.

Otherwise, keep your mouth shut.

John 8:7
If any one of you is without sin, let him be the first to throw a stone.

Rule
95

Every day do something
you love to do.
Eat a strawberry sundae while
taking a hot bath.
It sustains character.

1 Timothy 6:17
Put [your] hope in God, who richly provides us with everything for our enjoyment.

Remember the first principle concerning money: it all belongs to God.

Ecclesiastes 5:19
When God gives . . . wealth and possessions . . . this is a gift of God.

Praise God. You are his.

1 Peter 2:9
. . .[you are] a people belonging to God, that you may declare praises of him who called you out of darkness into his wonderful light.

Pay your bills on time.

Romans 13:7
If you owe taxes, pay taxes.

Be aware of evil, and fight against it. But dwell on the good.

Philippians 4:8
. . .whatever is true, whatever is noble, whatever is right, whatever is pure, whatever is lovely, whatever is admirable—if anything is excellent or praiseworthy— think about such things.

If you are the leader, lead.

1 Corinthians 12:4
There are different kinds of gifts, but the same Spirit.

If you are a follower, follow.

1 Corinthians 12:5
There are different kinds of service, but the same Lord.

Rule

102

Be what the Lord loves.

Proverbs 6:16-19

There are six things the LORD hates—seven that are detestable to him: haughty eyes, a lying tongue, hands that shed innocent blood, a heart that devises wicked schemes, feet that are quick to rush into evil, a false witness who pours out lies and a man who stirs up dissension among brothers.

Rule 103

Keep a prayer journal.
You will be amazed at
God's work in your life.

Matthew 26:41
Watch and pray so that you will not fall into temptation.

Show your children you love them— just the way they are.

Romans 15:7
Accept one another.

Get enough sleep.

Joshua 21:44
The LORD gave them rest.

Never upstage.
Let someone else enjoy
the spotlight.

Proverbs 3:27
Do not withhold good from those who deserve it.

Let anger subside
before you take action.

Proverbs 29:11
A fool gives full vent to his action.

Keep an open mind.

Psalm 119:104
I gain understanding from your precepts.

Discuss.
Don't quarrel.

2 Timothy 2:23
Don't have anything to do with foolish and stupid arguments because you know they produce quarrels.

Live beyond reproach.

Philippians 3:17
Join with others in following my example, brothers, and take note of those who live according to the pattern we gave you.

Rule

111

Provide a sense of continuity
for your children.
Be an island of sanity
in the sea of life's turmoil.

Psalm 40:2
He set my foot on a rock and gave me a firm place to stand.

Trace your genealogy.

Deuteronomy 32:7
Remember the days of old; consider the generations long past.

Pass on your family history.

Deuteronomy 32:7
Ask your father and he will tell you.

Resist giving advice about Sabbath observance or proper church attire.

Luke 13:15
The Lord answered him, "You hypocrites! Doesn't each of you on the Sabbath untie his ox and donkey from the stall and lead it out to give it water?"

Read the fine print.

Joshua 23:6
Be careful to obey all that is written.

Do not spend your life earning your children's inheritance.

Ecclesiastes 2:21

For a man may do his work with wisdom, knowledge, and skill, and then he must leave all he owns to someone who has not worked for it. This too is meaningless and a great misfortune.

Keep disappointments in perspective.

Revelation 3:19

Those whom I love I rebuke and discipline.

Rule
118

Honor a stay-at-home mom.
She accepts the most demanding
job, receives the smallest paycheck,
and gets the least credit.

Proverbs 31
The virtuous woman.

FT. & IN.
INCHES

12FT.

MADE IN U.S.A.

1 2 3 4 5 6 7

Rule

119

When you are new to an organization, resist telling its members ways to improve. A lot was accomplished before you arrived.

Amos 5:13
Therefore the prudent man keeps quiet.

BP 021965

2   3   4   5   6   7   8

Be noble.

Luke 18:15

But the seed on good soil stands for those with a noble and good heart, who hear the word, retain it, and by persevering produce a crop.

Memorize the Ten Commandments.

Proverbs 3:1

My son, do not forget my teaching, but keep my commands in your heart.

Rule
122

Never seek revenge. Those who believe only in "an eye for an eye and a tooth for a tooth" end up blind and toothless.

Deuteronomy 32:35
It is mine to avenge; I will repay.

Recognize insignificant details. Then, ignore them.

Colossians 2:8
See to it that no one takes you captive through hollow and deceptive philosophy.

Concentrate on what really matters.

Matthew 6:24
No one can serve two masters.

Be able to play the second fiddle well.

Proverbs 25:27
It is not good to eat too much honey, nor is it honorable to seek one's own honor.

Respect your elders.

Proverbs 16:31
Gray hair is a crown of splendor; it is attained by a righteous life.

Ponder.

Ecclesiastes 7:13
Consider what God has done.

Get off the merry-go-round of materialism.

Ecclesiastes 2:11
Yet when I surveyed all that my hands had done and what I had toiled to achieve,
everything was meaningless, a chasing after the wind;
nothing was gained under the sun.

Rule
129

Refuse to talk negatively about others.

Proverbs 17:4
A wicked man listens to evil lips; a liar pays attention to a malicious tongue.

Rule

130

Know the difference between grain and chaff.

Ecclesiastes 7:21
Do not pay attention to every word people say—or you may hear your servant cursing you.

Tithe.

Proverbs 3:9
Honor the LORD with your wealth, with the firstfruits of all your crops.

Examine your life.

Lamentations 3:40
Let us examine our ways and test them, and let us return to the LORD.

At some point say "enough is enough."

Ecclesiastes 5:10
Whoever loves money never has money enough, whoever loves wealth is never satisfied with his income.

Let your virtues speak for themselves.

Proverbs 13:9
The light of the righteous shines brightly.

Console.

Psalm 94:19
Your consolation brought joy to my soul.

Never cry over spilled anything.
It's done. Move on.

Isaiah 43:18
Do not dwell on the past.

Never presume to know the spiritual condition of a fellow believer.

Matthew 7:1
Do not judge, or you too will be judged.

Set your course.

Hebrews 12:1
Throw off everything that hinders and the sin that so easily entangles, and let us run with perseverance the race marked out for us.

Be one of the few
who can keep a secret.

Proverbs 11:13
But a trustworthy [person] keeps a secret.

Cultivate a sense of humor.

Ecclesiastes 3:4
A time to weep, and a time to laugh.

Rule
141

Say the three most difficult words:
"I was wrong."

Luke 13:5
Unless you repent, you too will all perish.

Set limits.

1 Corinthians 6:12
*Everything is permissible for me—but not everything is beneficial.
Everything is permissible for me—but I will not be mastered by anything.*

Avoid placing blame.
(It may fall on you.)

John 8:7
If any one of you is without sin, let him be the first to throw a stone at her.

Let your children see you pray on your knees.

Matthew 5:16
In the same way, let your light shine before men, that they may see your good deeds.

Never shirk a task.

Jonah 1

Invest more time and effort on inner beauty than outer.

Proverbs 31:30

Grace is deceptive and beauty is fleeting, but the worman who fears the Lord is to be praised.

Overlook faults in others.

Psalm 19:12

Forgive my hidden faults.

Admit your shortcomings.

James 1:14
But each one is tempted by his own evil desire.

Don't be stingy.

Proverbs 28:22
A stingy man is eager to get rich and is unaware that poverty awaits him.

Rule
150

Know when the horse is dead,
then get off it.

Titus 3:9
Avoid foolish controversies . . . and arguments and quarrels about the law,
because these are unprofitable and useless.